I am Unicorn born of the sun
who roams the hidden places
who rides the cloud
who tames the beast.

I drink the still waters.

I see the center.

I am the lawless one
whose name is Submission.

I am the spearpoint of truth.

I am the master of your dreams
and desires.

I am you

THIS IS YOUR BOOK & YOUR STORY

The Unicorn Notebook

ILLUMINATED·BY·MICHAEL·GREEN

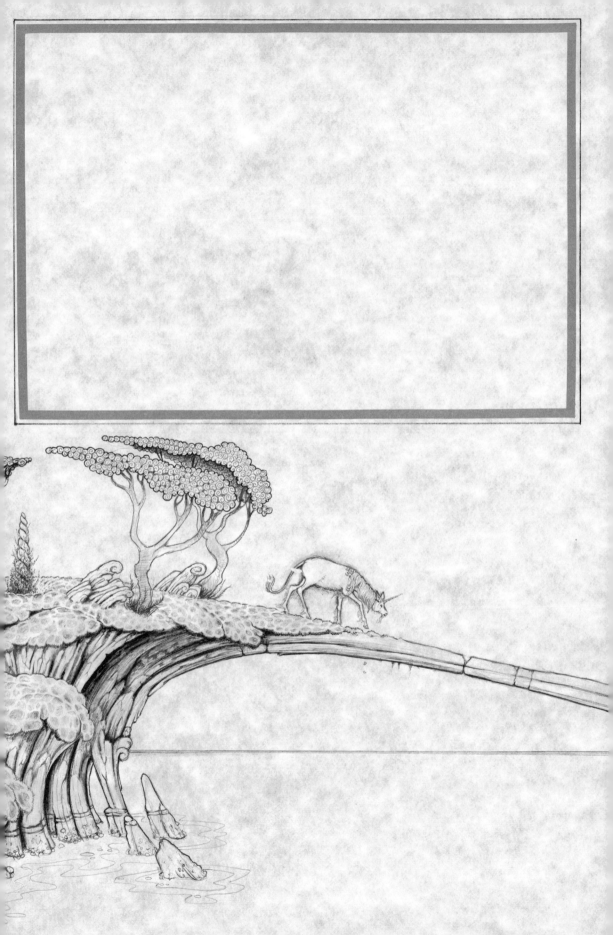

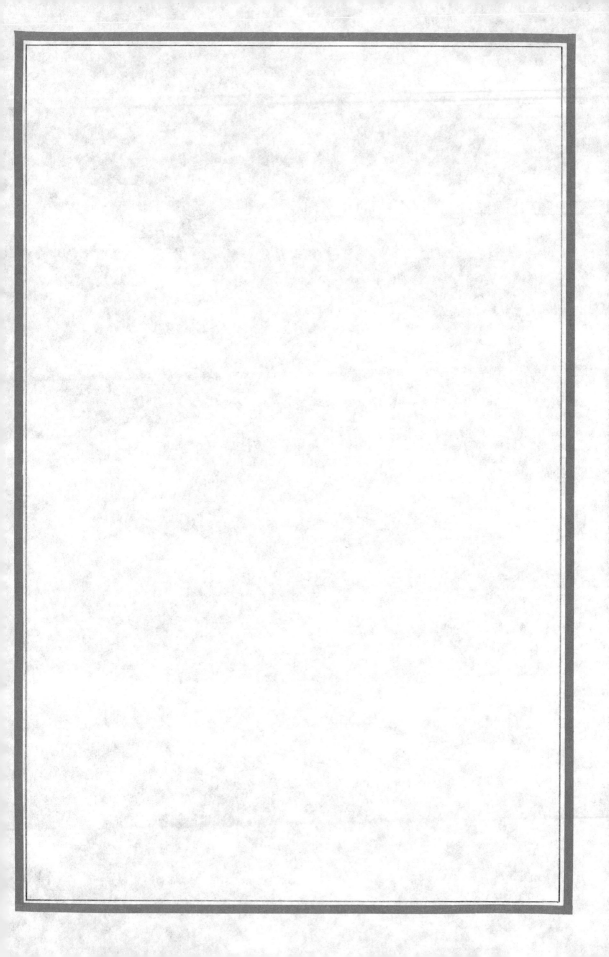